The New Town On ᶠs
— The Story Of Cliftonville

Volume One – Mainly until 1940

by NICK EVANS

Bygone Publishing

FRONT COVER PHOTO: Northdown Road at the junction with Godwin Road c1912.

BACK COVER PHOTO: The Oval bandstand and lawns c1925.

Contents

Author's introduction

Class conscious Victorians thrilled at the chance of leaving the grimy city for lungfuls of healthy sea air but to say you had spent your holiday in downmarket Margate was too much to bear. Instead, just a mile or so up the road from this brash, cockney influenced fleshpot was developed a new town on the cliffs – Cliftonville, to become its cheek by jowel, but far better behaved, neighbour.

Cliftonville was able to provide the best of everything by the end of the 19th century – top class hotels, smart shops selling all that an affluent lady or gentleman might need and, no less importantly, the opportunity to see and be seen on its miles of sunny promenades. It was said that a lady would need up to 40 dresses at her disposal to see her through the summer season.

For the more adventurous, there was the chance of a sedate swim in the sea – after changing into some concealing swimwear in a horsedrawn bathing machine, of course.

The tone changed after the First World War and by the 1930s, with the arrival of holidays with pay, Cliftonville had become more mainstream with new facilities like the Lido being developed to provide non-stop entertainment through the day, much of it under cover.

I felt inspired by the photos and memories I saw on the Cliftonville Nostalgia Facebook page and when I embarked on this project, it quickly became obvious that a single book would not do justice to the story of Cliftonville. This volume charts the town's early history until the Second World War while a second volume, continuing from 1945 to recent times, is already in preparation.

It's been a delight to research Cliftonville's story and I'm extremely grateful to all those who have supplied information and kindly allowed me to reproduce photos and postcards, many of which are more than 100 years old, from their collections. I hope you enjoy reading my book and it helps you gain a greater understanding of what Cliftonville was once like and may yet, hopefully, become again.

Nick Evans
Whitstable
May 2021

Cliftonville's early days and boom years

The concept of a new town dates back more than 150 years – and Cliftonville, just a mile or so up the road from Margate, was among the first.

Despite more than a century's worth of growth and urban sprawl where anybody would be forgiven for seeing Margate and Cliftonville as one and the same, the latter has done well to maintain some individuality.

Cliftonville has played, variously over the decades, the triple role of holiday resort, shopping centre and residential haven.

There is no historical connotation for the name. One source tells us it is merely descriptive; another refers to 'the town on the cliffs'. Yet at a time when Margate was fashionable for its bathing rooms – offering hot or cold fresh water for sea bathing – one of the best known was the Clifton Baths.

Records show there was a Cliftonville estate being built in 1865 and that the stately Cliftonville Hotel opened in 1868.

Thought to be the earliest illustration of Cliftonville is an 1860 engraving of Magdala Villas, seen from Edgar Road, which became the first 12 shops of Northdown Road. The remaining two of three Gouger's Mills, on the right, were pulled down in 1875, the third having been lost some years earlier in a fire started as a diversionary tactic by smugglers keen to land their illicit goods on the local beaches.

Although some locals may disagree, today's Cliftonville is regarded as stretching from Zion Place, just south of the Winter Gardens, beyond Palm Bay to the boundary with Broadstairs. Before the name was current it was known as New Town though Sir Robert

Peel (twice Prime Minister and founder of the modern police service) once owned so much of the land here that it was called, for a short time, Peel Town, despite his death in 1850.

A guide book of 1900 states: "Since Cliftonville has more desirable connections than Margate, the Cliftonville and New Town quarters having nothing in common with the regions sacred to the daytripper, the name spread gradually to include pre-1868 parts of Margate."

There used to be a Cliftonville at Brighton and it is said the Sussex resort was 'not at all pleased' at the flattery implied by Margate's imitation and took prompt action to rename its area as Hove.

Butlin's St George's Hotel made an imposing backdrop to a relaxing game of bowls on the green opposite when this photo was captured in 1982.

The Cliftonville Hotel was in the forefront of a growth of smart hotels that were to make the area famous to generations of visitors. There was also the Queen's Highcliffe, diagonally opposite, both buildings having disappeared in post Second World War developments. Long gone too are the former Butlin's hotels, the St George's, Grand and Norfolk Hotels, having made way for modern blocks of apartments and sheltered accommodation.

Some people can still recall the evenings when hotel guests wore dinner jackets and evening gowns and it was a memorable sight for passers-by to enjoy the grandeur apparent at every dining room window while the meal progressed. Facing the site of the Grand Hotel, the Oval bandstand and lawns still exist. Although not oval shaped, it was long famous for hosting contrasting events such as local band performances, beauty contests and all-in wrestling tournaments.

In the 1920s a concert party played the Oval during busy summer seasons – it was the renowned Fred Wildon's Margate Entertainers and in 1926 one of its troupe was a rising young comedian called Arthur Askey.

In his memoirs written during the mid 1970s Arthur recalled: "There were no microphones in those days, so one had to be heard over the sound of the sea, the children, dogs barking, cars hooting and even the occasional plane on a pleasure flight. That is where I learned to project my voice – a lost art these days."

Nearer the Margate end was the Lido pleasure centre. In the immediate post-war era its 1,500 seat theatre was a haven for performers making a name for themselves on the summer season circuit. Some would rise to become

Pettman's Bathing Station at the base of the cliffs of Newgate Gap c1910. Most people hired their bathing costumes in those days as well as the tent in which to change.

big names – including comedians Benny Hill and Reg Varney who would later have their own shows on TV.

During the 19th century there was one man in particular who realised Cliftonville's potential for the bathing fraternity – his name was Thomas Pettman. An employee of the Clifton Baths (which later became the Lido), he had the foresight to lease a part of the foreshore. He set up a new bathing station at Newgate

Gap and found success in hiring out bathing machines. The station comprised a large platform at the base of the cliffs, nicknamed Pettman's splashboard, and could seat dozens of visitors in deck chairs. Many people, not having swimming costumes of their own, hired them from here. One or two of these not-very-flattering outfits survive to this day as novelties of a bygone era!

A German who liked to fly the Union Jack and the White Ensign was Friedrich Hodges, an eccentric who owned a London gin distillery and a private fire brigade. He erected a 128 feet high flagstaff from which to fly his colours at Palm Bay and it quickly became a familiar local landmark, featuring on many contemporary postcards.

Benjamin Baker and his donkeys await their next duty offering rides to beachgoers at Newgate Gap c1890. Note the original footbridge erected by Friedrich Hodges.

By 1861 an iron bridge, which Hodges paid for, had been completed at Newgate Gap to help people reach the spot. At the opening, it was unveiled with a banner bearing the Latin words 'Pro bono publico' (for the good of the public). When the flagstaff decayed, the council put up a new one in 1899, such was the popularity of the spot.

By 1907, the iron bridge too was proving inadequate and again, the council stumped up the cash for a new one. This, in turn, was replaced 96 years later by Thanet District Council which had already replaced Hodges' and Sackett's Bridges over the slipways in 1993 leading down to the beach at Palm Bay.

Traditionally, Cliftonville's main shopping centre has been Northdown Road. For many years the range and quality of shops helped set apart Cliftonville from its more bourgeoisie neighbour, Margate. Bobby's department store, for example, was the local equivalent of Harrod's until its closure in 1973. Many family run businesses have kept up a tradition of service appreciated by residents and visitors over the years.

The late 1960s saw Cliftonville expand beyond Palm Bay to the edge of Broadstairs with the building of the Northdown Park Estate, complete with its own shops and pub, adding a new dimension to Cliftonville as Cliftonville did for Margate.

At the heart of Cliftonville though have been the roads of guest houses and small private hotels. Nearly all were 'minutes from the seafront and shops' catering for a thriving holiday market in the pre-package tour era. Like many resorts, Cliftonville suffered badly when the lure of guaranteed sunshine proved too much to resist and social deprivation ultimately made its presence felt.

It's all too easy to write off the place now, but for those who feel able to look up at some of the distinctive buildings of Northdown Road, there is still some grandeur trying hard to shine through the tarnish.

The domed building in this view was Bobby's department store until its closure in 1973. Ten years later, when this photo was taken, part of it had become Fads DIY and paint shop. For some, Bobby's closure marked the beginning of a slow decline along Northdown Road.

Promenading along the foreshore

21498. FORENESS BAY. CLIFTONVILLE.

Foreness Bay is the beach to the east of Palm Bay, seen in the background of this 1930s view by Judges postcards. Lines of canvas changing tents and a neatly finished café dominate the promenade but there is plenty of space for fun on the sand while the tide is out. On the clifftop beyond, with a newly built art deco style house beside it, is the dark brick building of Goodwin House Girls' School.

Foreness Point is not only the eastern most point of Cliftonville but the end of the Thames Estuary and when this postcard was mailed in September 1927 it was undeveloped compared to the views of later years. The building on the point was a Coastguard station while the white structure on the right was the unusually named Hydrophone Tea Lounge. A hydrophone is an underwater microphone that detects and records the sounds of the ocean – so how this area of clifftop was given the name is uncertain.

PALM BAY GARDENS, CLIFTONVILLE.

36.

The actual copy of the postcard seen here was posted in June 1945, less than a month after VE Day marking the end of the Second World War but the photo was taken some 12 years earlier. While perhaps not at their best, the gardens still look tidy to an approaching gaggle of promenaders taking the sea air. The buildings in the centre are the Koh-I-Noor Café and wine lodge.

A warm dry summer has perhaps taken its toll on the Palm Bay bowling green, seen here just before the Second World War. The bridge over the slipway to the bay itself survives but an old boat house, partly in view here, fell down during a storm in December 2019. The beach is far from crowded, offering a haven of calm in contrast to the main sands of more raucous Margate.

At the end of a bracing 1.5 mile stroll from Margate, the Koh-I-Noor Café, seen here in 1912, offered welcome refreshment for many before the return journey. Ice creams and dainty teas would be served but there was the option to enjoy something stronger as it also sold a variety of wines and spirits. It's worth noting the next nearest hostelry was several minutes walk away.

Putting Course, "Koh-I-Noor," Palm Bay Margate.

Sinking a few holes on the putting green before adjourning to the Koh-I-Noor Café or wine lodge afterwards was a pleasant way of spending one's holiday time in the years before the Second World War. Both the putting green and the larger of the two buildings were lost long ago but the smaller building survives as a popular café today.

CLIFTONVILLE, The Tennis Courts 1003

Adjoining Palm Bay's bowling green on its western side were, and still are, a number of public tennis courts, evidently popular in this 1920s view, both for players and spectators. Hotels and large houses were gradually springing up along the seafront by this time – but not nearly as numerous as in the years following – yet we can see open fields in the distance towards Botany Bay. Much of the land at Palm Bay was owned by Simon Van Den Bergh, who had made his fortune in butter and margarine. In 1924 he sold the ground to developers who went on to build the avenues, including Leicester and Gloucester, of the Palm Bay Estate.

Wealthy German born eccentric Friedrich Hodges first erected a flagstaff at Palm Bay in 1861 and it quickly became a focal point for promenaders. A large Union Jack and White Ensign would be flown from the mast and were visible for miles around. The land was gifted to the town in October 1870 by George Pitt in memory of his late father who had been among the many to enjoy a daily walk to the spot. The gift included the seating, 660 feet of iron fencing and 12 assorted cannon. We see Hodges' flagstaff in 1929.

V.373-5 CLIFTONVILLE. FLAGSTAFF PROMENADE RAPID PHOTO E C

Under the watchful eye of their father, a group of small boys clambers over the cannon at the flagstaff and consider which passing ship they might like to fire upon, if they could, in this scene captured c1907. The cannon were later buried for safety at the outbreak of the Second World War in 1939 and only raised once more in early 1982 for a much needed restoration.

THE BUNGALOW, CLIFTONVILLE.

THE BUNGALOW REFRESHMENTS

By the time this image was captured in 1937, the Bungalow refreshment gardens had grown to a considerable size and would have been catering for hundreds of people every day in the summer season. Clearly visible are the four lamp standards denoting the corners of Hodges Bridge over the slipway to the beach below, one of two access points to the sands in this vicinity.

The domed Palm Bay Café which, like those at Foreness and Walpole Bays stood on raised wooden platforms in front of the cliffs, looks imposing in this scene captured during the inter-wars era. Canvas sided changing huts were readily available as were deck chairs, judging by the two stacks on the sand. Sadly, the café was completely destroyed by the storm of early 1953.

The Armistice which brought an end to the horrors of the First World War had been signed only six months earlier when this postcard of swimmers enjoying a dip at Walpole Bay was posted in May 1919. Conspicuous by their absence, there are no bathing machines in the water, just plenty of people splashing around, a sign perhaps there was less need to be self-conscious in swimwear?

Open sea bathing is nature's tonic, proclaims the sign on the end of Walpole Bay's café and pavilion sometime in the late 1920s, serving holidaymakers since the end of the 19th century. Like the café at Palm Bay, the entire structure was smashed to pieces during the 1953 storm which lashed most of England's east coast but was rebuilt a short time after to a different style.

WALPOLE BAY, CLIFTONVILLE. VIEW FROM THE AIR.   M. 6.

Walpole Bay's tidal pool was built by Margate Corporation for £7,000 and opened in June 1937. It used scrap rails from the newly closed Isle of Thanet Tramway to reinforce the one ton concrete blocks needed in its construction. The three sided pool measured no less than four acres and was seven feet deep at the end furthest from the cliffs. Working by day and night according to the tides, building the pool was seen as an engineering feat at the time. This was duly recognised when it was given grade two listing in August 2014. English Heritage said: "As a structure, the Walpole Bay tidal pool has social historical interest as it provided an improvement to sea bathing at the period of the greatest popularity of the English seaside."

THE BOWLING GREENS, WALPOLE BAY, CLIFTONVILLE   15673

Leaning out of a bedroom window at the front of St George's Hotel, an intrepid cameraman has a grand view of the bowling greens opposite and the nearby Walpole Bay Hotel. Until the early 1980s, a weather station by the bowls pavilion recorded the hours of sunshine – and rainfall – used by the council and local newspapers in publicising how much sunnier Cliftonville and Margate were compared to other seaside resorts.

THE QUEENS PROMENADE, CLIFTONVILLE

E 03066

Taken at the point where Queen's Promenade would later run into the easterly Prince's Walk, a young lady is striding purposefully, bag in hand, perhaps to meet a suitor? Behind her, a bath chair user has stopped to chat with friends. The large building beyond was originally four hotels, the Dalmeny, the Queen's, Kimber's and the Highcliffe, in the very early years of the 20th century.

Set in Ethelbert Crescent, the Oval bandstand we know today was created in 1897, along with deckchair seating for 2,000 people on its terraces. The site had previously been a playing field for the boys of Albion House prep school in Sweyn Road until the death of headmaster Charles Schimmelman. The land was then bought by Jacob Lewis who allowed a temporary bandstand to be built in 1890. In this scene, an Edwardian concert party is in full swing entertaining a decent sized audience.

During the period between the First and Second World Wars, the Oval was at the heart of Cliftonville's entertainments with concert parties proving popular in the summer season. Among the performers cutting their teeth here was comedian Arthur Askey who appeared in 1926, the same year the Oval was used for the official opening of nearby Prince's Walk by the Prince of Wales, later to be the Duke of Windsor after abdicating as King Edward VIII. We can see from this 1930s aerial view, the Oval is, in reality, a circle.

The bridge at Newgate Gap, accessed by a slipway cut through the chalk off Ethelbert Crescent, has been a popular subject for several postcard publishers since the 1860s. In that time there have been three bridges over the gap, the first built by Friedrich Hodges to enable promenaders to reach the flagstaff at Palm Bay, the second erected by Margate Corporation in 1907 to mark its golden jubilee and when that was finally declared unsafe more than 90 years later, Thanet District Council commissioned a replacement which was opened in 2003.

1   CLIFTONVILLE. — View from the High Cliffe. — LL.

Contrast the two views of the original and second bridges over Newgate Gap taken by French postcard publisher LL in the early twentieth century. Above: The first bridge, made of iron, was a fairly basic affair, but even so lasted more than 40 years. Left: The 1907 bridge was a far more robust construction, better able to withstand heavy-footed promenaders and salty sea air.

30   CLIFTONVILLE (Margate). — Queen's Promenade. — LL.

The beach scene of Newgate Gap, c1904, shows one end of the raised platform of Pettman's Bathing Station which stretched along to Walpole Bay. The station offered extensive changing facilities, refreshments and horsedrawn wagon rides to bathing machines. The original bridge has been braced by now and we can make out the artificial rockery and tunnel under the road beyond it, built in 1901 by respected landscaper James Pulham & Son using its own type of cement called Pulhamite.

Donkey rides were an added pleasure for younger beachgoers to Newgate Gap in the years immediately before the First World War and their progress along the sands would have added to the vista enjoyed by those standing on the new bridge above. The angle of the view emphasises the bridge's sturdiness and reassures people that British industry had built something which would last.

'Palm Bay pleases the public' proclaims the rear end of the van delivering goods to the Cave beach shop on the left side of the incline to the sands sometime in the early 1930s. Cigarettes and Margate rock are on sale in Pettman's outlet on the other side. Right: The scene of the steps at the top of the slope, looking to Margate, shows off the Pulhamite facing to good effect.

Gap Steps, Cliftonville, Margate

10572   MARGATE, GOING BATHING   ROTARY PHOTO. E.C.

Either the young lady has changed her mind about taking a ride to a bathing machine or she is queue jumping! We get a clear look at a wagon used to take bathers to the covered machines along the water's edge of Newgate Gap. They could walk the plank to the wagon, climb in for the ride and clamber into their machine, all on the same level without getting their clothing wet.

Within the photograph, the advertisement reads:

CHARLOTTE PETTMAN'S
ORIGINAL
SEA-WATER BATHS,

THE ONLY ENTRANCE TO
CHARLOTTE PETTMAN'S BATHS

NEW TOWN, MARGATE
(Two minutes' walk from Dalby Square.)
Entrance: DOWN THE COASTGUARD CUTTING
Under the Bridge.

The BATHING MACHINES are superior to all others for
CLEANLINESS and VENTILATION, and the
PURITY OF THE SEA-WATER IS UNSURPASSED

A neat line of bathing machines awaits swimmers at Pettman's Bathing Station, Newgate Gap c1903. The main structure's roof denotes its New Town, rather than Cliftonville, location. Pettman's splashboard, as it was nicknamed, was opened by Thomas Pettman around 1855 after he leased the beach from the Marquis of Conyngham for £3,000. Thomas' daughter Charlotte, widowed after her husband and cousin William died young in 1865, had already been managing the station for some time but assumed sole ownership upon her father's death in 1886. Charlotte died in 1918 when her son Frederick took over control. He later sold the station to the council in 1933.

10572 1   MARGATE. FORT.   ROTARY PHOTO, EC

Some 15 years before John Henry Iles bought it in the early 1920s, the Clifton Baths was a very different place from what it would later become, catering for a more middle class clientele who appreciated the virtues of bathing in heated salt water, followed by a thorough working over from an unforgiving masseur or masseuse. The chimney beyond the Baths Saloon exists to this day as the familiar Lido beacon.

Beachgoers wait their turn to clamber inside a bathing machine at the Clifton Baths c1907 – no high rise wagon to spare you wet clothing! The Clifton Baths was made of several underground spaces and one, a wide spiral tunnel enabling bathing machines to be hauled to street level, would lead to the entire site becoming grade two listed some 100 years after this image was recorded.

Loving a leisurely life at the Lido

Where Dreamland was mainly designed for the kiss me quick, squeeze me slow day tripper, so the Lido, just a mile up the road in Cliftonville, was aimed at a more select class of visitor staying in the area for a week or two.

John Henry Iles realised quite early on this was a market which needed to be catered for. Shortly after getting Dreamland up and running in 1920 he bought the Clifton Baths Estate, a genteel sort of place which could trace its origins back a further 100 years when it had been frequented by the 'nobility and gentry resorting to Margate'.

The entrance to the Clifton Baths Estate, as it was properly known, soon after it was purchased by John Henry Iles. The site would not become known as the Lido until 1938.

The estate was especially well known to generations for its hot salt water baths. Its links with the past were many. Great caverns, honeycombed with passages, had been cut into the cliffs and once offered a hiding place to local smugglers. These were the result of many hours hard labour which were sometimes ill rewarded.

One gang made the mistake of burrowing too far upwards and found themselves in the kitchen of the revenue officer's cottage!

When Iles purchased the estate, it came complete with a funicular cliff railway, which had been installed just before the First World War, a cinema and the Joywheel ride. This was soon transferred to Dreamland and renamed the Lunar ride. In the years that followed, Iles spent £120,000 improving and rebuilding the estate with a cliff top sun terrace, bandstand and bars spread over three levels. An indoor warm sea water pool was the only one in Thanet, open from Easter to October and 'constantly attended by a highly skilled instructor'.

By 1925 Iles had leased a stretch of the foreshore from Margate Corporation and had embarked on a £60,000 programme to build a vast open air swimming pool.

The pool would be big enough to accommodate nearly 1,000 swimmers, with changing rooms and plenty of space for sitting, sunbathing and enjoying drinks afterwards – exactly what the paying public now wanted.

At 250 feet by 150 feet and depth graduating from two feet in the shallows to nine feet, sea water was drawn in through four large sluices at high tides. Around 1,300 tons of cement and 10,000 tons of ballast were used to construct the pool. Some 3,000 people could sit and enjoy the antics from terraced seating – or amphitheatre as it was properly known – set into the cliff edge. Close by, there was a huge dressing room with 400 changing cubicles. This was later extended to 800 with plunge, shower and foot baths.

A young girl was ceremoniously pushed into the pool as the first swimmer at the official opening by the Mayor of Margate, Cllr Mrs MHS Hatfeild, on 24 June 1927 – immediately followed by a typical British summer drenching which saw the entire party adjourn to the new French themed Café Normandie for an early lunch.

How the Clifton Baths Estate looked in a drawing from 1927 soon after the swimming pool's completion. The familiar beacon and funicular railway can be clearly seen.

Costumed waitresses gather for a group photo around a newly created bandstand in the French bar during the 1937 season.

A corner of the Jolly Tar Tavern in the mid 1930s. A nautical style welcome awaited willing customers in search of refreshment.

Later, three maroons were fired over the pool – for the King, the Mayor and Margate. This was followed by an exhibition of diving, boxing and wrestling on rafts by local clubs and a life saving display by local police.

For years after the pool would be open for much of the day during the summer season, closing at around midnight after evenings of moonlit swimming with appropriate mood music. The Clifton Baths changed its name to the Lido in 1938, prompting one of those awkward unknowns – should it be pronounced Leedo or Liedo? Various dictionaries suggest the former but to this day, you can hear both uttered in any conversation about the place.

Meanwhile on top of the cliffs, there emerged a giant new theatre for 1930. With seating for 1,500 and a sliding roof which would be opened during show intervals, it became a renowned venue on the summer show circuit, giving many up and coming performers an invaluable chance to hone their skills.

The theatre replaced the old

cinema, a wooden building dating back to 1910 that had opened originally as the Electric Theatre before becoming the Clifton Cinema. An advertisement in the town guide of 1911 boasts: 'Latest films – Continuous show – Programme

A painting commemorating the pool's official opening. The original hung in the office of pleasure centre manager Arthur Ashwood for many years.

changed daily'. Music was played on the latest concert gramophone equipment – usually the Grenadier and Coldstream Guards – during the intervals. Seat prices for adults were 6d and 3d and children were admitted for 3d and 2d each.

Publicity for the cinema in 1912 announced it was: 'The only theatre in Thanet using the stereoscopic screen, assuring steadiness and brilliancy' and by 1920 boasted: 'A fine new sunbrite screen, the largest and brightest pictures in town'.

The Clifton cinema was a popular venue for around 20 years but didn't survive the death blow dealt by the arrival of talking pictures. A decision was taken not to wire it for sound, leaving manager Jack Binns, who also managed Dreamland's cinema, with only one venue to promote.

The gentlemen's hairdressing salon of the Clifton Baths soon after completion in the early 1930s. The ladies' salon was just as well appointed.

Also during the early 1930s ladies and gentlemen's hairdressing salons were constructed along this top level nearest the Ethelbert Crescent side. Ladies were assured: 'Specialist staff have been engaged from leading establishments, highly skilled in all branches of the profession, including permanent waving.'

For the men, no expense had been spared in making their salon the finest and best equipped in the district. Comfort and cleanliness were everywhere in evidence, promotional brochures insisted.

Nearby were 50 private bathrooms serving medical and hot sea water baths. Each one had been fitted with marble floors and walls while the ozone filled waters 'continually helped cure rheumatism, sciatica and nervous disorders'. These would feature at the Lido at least until the outbreak of war.

An aquarium and mini zoo would replace the baths in the immediate post war era and survive for much of the 1950s. Filled with exotic tropical and coldwater fish plus a host of reptiles and even a few monkeys, this attraction was spread out on two levels. Among the keepers who cared for the animals was Gerald Durrell, later a famed naturalist, author, and founder in 1959 of the Jersey Zoo. He was a relief keeper in 1951.

The tropical aquarium and snake house frontage soon after opening at the Lido in 1948. Replacing the old baths, it survived for much of the following decade.

The bars were given a makeover during the 1930s. All had a theme of one kind or another. Largest was the Cliff Café. Originally designed to accommodate just 80 people in the early 1920s, it was extended to seat 1,000 in comfort. It provided an ideal vantage point from which to enjoy the sea views and pool scenes. Orchestras would play throughout the day and night.

The Café Normandie was decorated after the old style of the French region and was home to various orchestras for dancing during the thirties. The idea of something French, foreign and therefore immediately exciting was carried through to the French bar on the swimming pool level. Murals recalled the days of pirates on the high seas while the bar stools were made from the screws of old French wine presses.

Seafaring was more prominent in the Jolly Tar tavern where lobster pot lampshades jostled with oddments of ships' running and fishing gear. Typically, the Foc'sle Accordion Entertainers would be on hand to supply the nautical music.

Underneath the Café Normandie was the Café Basque, which at the time was thought to be the only one of its kind. This had been modelled on bars found in the Basque region of the Pyrenees. Rustic treatment of wood beams and stone arches helped build the intimate atmosphere.

The 1930s settled into a happy pattern of music in the square bandstand on the top level terrace – enjoyed from the comparative comfort of a deck chair – swimming in the pool and a show at night. Occasionally John Henry Iles, dressed in plus fours, could be

seen emerging from his Bentley to buy an ice cream and then enthusiastically pretend to conduct the band.

Among the first of many seasonal delights to come to the Clifton was On With The Show presented by Lawrence

The Café Basque bar, beneath the Café Normandie, offered a degree of initimacy and was modelled on those found in the Basque region of the Pyrenees during the 1930s.

Wright and featuring a cast of singers, dancers and a principal comedian – a formula that was typical of pre-television era summer shows around the country.

Although the performers were the same every night, their offerings were not. It was quite common for half a dozen versions of the programme to be produced setting out the changing bill – ideal for anyone staying in town to see something different every night of their holiday if they chose.

By the mid 1930s the Cliff Theatre was venue of the nightly Gay Parade shows, produced initially by Richard Jerome. Clearly, one wouldn't give a family show this title now – but these were more innocent times and the word gay meant fun. The Six Dancing Debutantes propped up the bill of soprano and soubrette singers, two comedians and a general entertainer, all supported by The Parade Orchestra.

During these years immediately before the Second

A late 1950s view inside the Lido's 1,500 seat theatre. During the interval of a show, sections of the roof would slide apart to let in fresh air and release cigarette smoke.

World War, one of the stars to appear here was Leslie Fuller. He was a fine example of local boy makes good. Born in Margate he once helped his father print papers and then sold them on the street.

During the First World War he served with the Huntingdonshire Cycling Battalion, having been posted to this unit because of his records and championships obtained for cycle racing. He later formed a concert party, the Ped'lers, which met with great success in the Army.

He returned to Margate in 1919 and set up the concert party in a tent adjoining the site. Later on, the troupe moved into the Clifton Concert Hall, now part of the Iles' owned estate.

Throughout the 1920s and early 1930s Leslie Fuller and the Ped'lers

Above: Although this photo dates from the post-war austerity period of the late 1940s, the Lido's sun deck and bandstand had changed little since redevelopment nearly 20 years before.

Left: Leisurely times at the Cliff Café sun terrace as seen c1935. It offered alfresco sun lounging or, in the evening, somewhere to relax after a swim in the vast open sea water pool.

were a familiar part of the estate. His talent for comedy took him in to films, making a total of 14 between 1930 and 1942. In 1934 the local papers reported he had signed a contract with one studio for £20,000 over five years.

Fatefully, in the late 1930s he set up a film production company with John Henry Iles as Chairman, based at Cricklewood in North London. This was the venture which would lead to Iles' eventual financial downfall.

Leslie's antics were followed by Lido audiences for years and the Ped'lers became one of Britain's best known concert parties. After 1945 he returned to Margate and became a local councillor. He also went back to the Lido for the 1947 season but was taken ill during the run and replaced by comedian Neville Kennard. The following year, still under 60, Leslie died.

Reg Varney was a hit of the post war era. The picture shows him as himself, left, and as his own ventriloquist's dummy.

In 1948 Hedley Claxton's Gaytime was presented in the theatre for the first time, running for the three seasons until 1950. Despite the austerity period, it was a more sophisticated show than the concert party style productions of earlier years. They are notable now in that two then rising comedians appeared on the bills. Topping the line up was Reg Varney, later to be better known in TVs On The Buses. One newspaper critic, Cecil Wilson of the Daily Mail, described Reg as 'a chirpy little cockney with long, lank, reddish hair, a Joe E Brown grin, a Bob Hope nose and a pair of impish eyes'.

For two of these three seasons, 1948 and 1950, one of the supporting artistes was a talented comedian who

A young Benny Hill appeared with Reg Varney in the 1948 and 1950 Gaytime summer shows.

would also become famous on TV – Benny Hill. Arguably, Benny went on to become more widely known internationally as his shows would be among the few which have been successful in America.

Seat prices for 1950 were 4/6d down to 3/6d, 2/6d and 1/6d. Or in today's money, 23p, 17p, 13p, and 7p!

The Lido suffered severely in the 1953 storm which lashed most of the east coast. The swimming pool, at the mercy of the raging waves, was extensively damaged.

Above: The Golden Garter saloon included a jailhouse and a set of gallows to quell the unruly element!

Left: Gunfight at the OK Corral or is it Boot Hill? Believe it or not the photo was taken outside the very doors of the Golden Garter in 1965 – so ran the caption for this publicity picture of the gun-toting cowboys starring in the wild west show. The hombré in the big white stetson is Sheriff Danny Arnold.

Just a small section of the damage caused by the 1953 storm. All levels of the Lido were badly affected.

Quick on the draw with Sheriff Danny Arnold in the 1960s. Chances are the girls were winners of that week's pool parade.

The Café Normandie, opposite the pool entrance was wrecked when a 20ft slab of concrete hurtled into it. The café was not rebuilt. In its place emerged the Golden Garter saloon which was, for many summers after, the home of a wild west show. Until the end of the 1960s this featured Sheriff Danny Arnold, show girls and a group of entertainers collectively known as the Vigilantes. Loud music, singing, the occasional shooting, a fully stocked bar and a jailhouse for the particularly unruly – as much for the cast as the paying audience – made this a memorable night out for many.

Danny really was a sheriff – he was a deputy of Bexar County, San Antonio, Texas, and more than once helped out his American bosses by following up leads in Britain.

It was said the Canadian born wild west expert got an income tax allowance for cigars which were all part of his professional image and he paid half a guinea each for the five cigars he smoked every day. In old money that was £2 15 shillings a day, an expensive habit for the era!

Ever the entertainer, he could never resist ending even the most casual of conversations with a quip such as: "Look out for those injuns!"

So-long Folks!

Sure hope to see you again

(Photo by courtesy of Isle of Thanet Gazette)

Above: An unusual view of a gunfight on the promenade outside the Golden Garter captured by the Isle of Thanet Gazette in the 1960s and used on the back page of the show's programme.

Left: The Sheriff, his Wild West Vigilantes and showgirls pose in the Golden Garter saloon in 1959.

The Lido was regularly packed on all levels to watch weekly bathing beauty contests throughout the 1950s, 1960s and 1970s. This photo serves to emphasise the scale and size of the place. Note the picture windows to keep the wind off the Sun Terrace.

The pool was in good order when this aerial view of the Lido was captured in the 1950s by the Isle of Thanet Gazette. Up to 1,000 people at a time could swim here. The sea water would be changed with overnight tides every few days during the season.

Making his mark with a new type of summer production, was Bunny Baron, who until his death in 1978 directed shows throughout the country. Lido Theatre audiences of the early fifties were able to see the quick speaking Londoner in the rollicking 'Sunshine and Smiles' for five seasons.

A period in which formal dress declined, it was all the more notable when worn. One man who gave a touch of the old days to Lido audiences was front of house manager Huntley Macdonald. A former professional actor, he was always to be seen wearing his dress suit, with neat red rose in the lapel, as customers were shown to their seats. Starting at the Lido just after the Second World War, Mac, as he was known, continued into the mid 1950s.

The Jamaica Bar was created at the Lido in 1973 and proved a mainstay of refreshment for those who preferred a lazy time in a deckchair.

Similar format shows continued after Bunny left, and by the early sixties stars whose names were already made were shining at the Lido Theatre.

They included Beryl Reid, 1960, Bill Maynard, 1961

and 1965, while the 1964 season starred Tommy Trinder. His ad-libbing skills were thoroughly tested on opening night. The theatre organ had broken down, putting the musical part of the show out of action while repairs were hurriedly carried out, leaving Tommy jesting on stage by himself for 35 minutes. The audience, none the wiser, assumed it was all part of his act.

Shows with a similar music plus comedy format continued for several years but the public appeared to be growing tired of the type of production they could see on TV. The management decided to try comedy plays for a couple of years, then a colourful Carnival On Ice show in 1973. For this, the entire stage was taken up by an ice tank taking 18 hours to freeze over before being skated upon.

Norman Wisdom, right of sign, and show promoter Martin Gates celebrate a full house at the Lido Theatre in 1975.

Charlie Drake gets the bird – 18 year old Elaine that is – in 1976.

In 1974 there was a return to musical with 'The Amazing Penny Whistle Show' and a similar format was kept for 1975 but with Norman Wisdom as the star. This was an excellent season for the Lido and house full boards were outside the theatre on many nights.

The following year comic Charlie Drake made a comeback from performing exile after a dispute with actors' union Equity. His 11 week season began in July and not long after he made national headlines when he announced his engagement to 18 year old chorus girl, Elaine Bird. The happy couple though did not marry. Appearing on the same bill was ventriloquist Roger de Courcey and his bear Nookie who had together recently won ITV talent show New Faces.

Bunny Baron made a return to the Lido in 1977 when he produced Take A Tripp 77 featuring Jack Tripp.

The Lido's Sun Terrace in 1980 – the penultimate season before closure. Family entertainment and music was led by Tony Savage.

Bunny said at the time he believed the basic show formula hadn't changed a great deal in the 20 plus years since he was last in Cliftonville but modern audiences now expected better value for money with greater originality, colour and artistry – all influences of TV. People wanted a show to move swiftly along rather than be held up with sketches.

Mounting costs of hiring celebrities and a shrinking economy forced the management to look harder at the summer shows in the Lido Theatre. The main summer show style changed in the late 1970s to end of the pier style entertainments under the titles of There'll Always Be An England which met with reasonable success, as did The Al Jolson Minstrel Show – a line up of now unfashionable black & white minstrels plus chorus girls. Hard work put in by the management and

The Old Time Music Hall line up of dancers for the 1980 season.

Comedian Tommy Trinder enjoyed a successful summer season at the Lido Theatre in 1979.

Photocall for the Al Jolson Minstrel Show cast with promoter Duggie Chapman in 1980. Blackened faces are much frowned upon now.

cast in 1978 paid off with a surge of seat sales for the theatre.

Wanting to win a younger audience to the centre, a new discotheque named Hades had been opened in August 1971. This was housed in the former dance cavern bar behind the theatre. Aimed strictly at the over 20s it was open in the summer from Thursday to Sunday from 9pm until 2am. Exotic dancers appeared on Thursday nights. A supper licence in the disco's restaurant saw doors actually open from 8pm. In the early 1980s, the name was changed to Colonel Bogey's, necessitated in part by an unwanted reputation for disorder.

Applying the finishing touches to the hand-painted soldiers adorning Colonel Bogey's nightclub, formerly Hades.

Out on the sun terrace organist Tony Savage entertained thousands of deck-chaired holidaymakers every summer for many years, while the Jamaica Bar, restyled for £10,000 in 1973, saw the arrival of Norris Leslie playing a three manual, 10 rank Lowrey Citation organ. Both Norris and Tony would be working hard seven days a week at the season's height to entertain.

Nearby was the Old Time Music Hall which had transferred in the late 1960s from Dreamland when Margate Estates sold out to Associated Leisure.

From 1970 the show was produced by and featured Al and Kathie Dene – 'Majestic Mancunians, masters of merriment and melody' – and their artistes. In 1973 their growing success and loyal following justified a

£12,000 makeover of the Cliff Café into the music hall's new summer base. Al and Kathie ran these shows until the end of the decade but music hall continued here in one form or another until the Lido's closure at the end of the 1981 season.

In July of that year Associated Leisure announced in a short press statement it had sold the complex to Golden Coast Amusements of Ilfracombe.

Things didn't work out for the new owners and despite some ambitious plans to rebuild the swimming pool into something more modern and meeting new safety standards, the Lido has been sold on more than once and has lain largely dormant ever since. The theatre, beginning to show signs of age even in the early 1980s, has long since been demolished. Only a difference in the colour of the tarmac surface marks the site. The pool was filled in years ago to become little more than an oversized sandpit.

Taken in 2000, the Lido's swimming pool had already been abandoned for nearly 20 years. Today, it is in considerably worse condition.

In the intervening 40 years, various developers and Thanet District Council have wrangled over what to do with the place. A snooker club and bar still operate but it's fair to say the rest of the Lido has been a sad blot on the local landscape, heightening the overall shabbiness of what was once a prosperous part of town.

A variety of plans have been put forward during the past four decades. One scheme would have seen the famous Lido beacon moved elsewhere in the complex to make way for a new block of flats, a 30 room hotel and leisure facilities. It also included a health and beauty village, three restaurants, a nightclub and a language school.

Outline planning permission was granted soon after, subject to an agreement between council and developer but this was not settled.

A second scheme, involving flats with shops and an entertainment venue, fell through when the developer's fortunes nosedived after another of its ventures stalled.

Hopes for a Lido renaissance rose once more when there was talk of a Sea Life Centre moving in but that came to nothing as well.

Meanwhile the buildings, particularly on promenade level, have been kept watertight and painted while the beacon was given a makeover in 2003.

In more recent times volunteers have formed themselves into a pressure group to successfully see much of the site become grade two listed. A spiral tunnel beneath the Lido, dating from the Clifton Bath's earliest days, down which horsedrawn bathing machines would have been hauled to the water's edge, proved a key element for the listing to be given.

Funding was awarded to the volunteers in 2019 to remove about 20 tons of rubbish and debris from the buildings – a herculean task. The £44,000 grant also paid for 3D laser scans of the site to be made to establish the site's current condition.

The Covid19 pandemic meant that further plans, particularly around seeking a share of central government regeneration funding, had to be temporarily shelved but the group is hopeful it can pick up again from 2021 onwards.

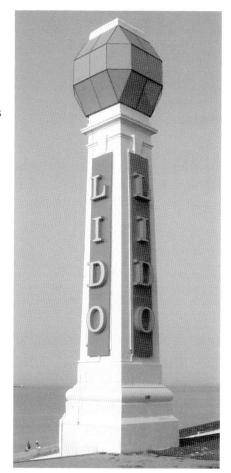

The Lido beacon was given an overhaul in 2003 and looked resplendent then.

Strolling through town and around

Cliff Terrace Cliftonville Nº 8461.

The Isle of Thanet Tramway had become an established part of the scenery of Cliftonville when this view along Cliff Terrace, taking in its rails and overhead wires, was caught around 1912. The shops stand opposite the Clifton Baths so would pick up a good passing trade – even the chemist would have done well offering patent medicines for holiday related conditions!

Cliftonville, Margate.

Just around the corner from the previous photo, Cliff Terrace opens out to give us one of Cliftonville's most familiar postcard views. This image dates from around 1908 and is still recognisable today thanks to the five storey Corner House shops and flats. When you see this view coming from Margate, you know you have definitely arrived in Cliftonville.

The shops in Cliff Terrace would have served a thriving community living close by in the early years of the twentieth century – not just visitors. A toy shop and bazaar, Post Office, restaurant and branch of DT Evans chemist ply their trade accordingly. Later, the residential properties in the corner of the terrace would be converted into more shops with flats above.

Zion Place. Margate

Today, for many people Zion Place marks the boundary between Cliftonville and Margate. The road has been straightened and widened since this Edwardian view was taken looking in the direction of Northdown Road. Bowden's florist is just in shot on the left while further away, the flat frontage of the Randolph Hotel stands out against the bay windows of the terraced houses.

Athelstan Road is, from the west, the first of a dozen roads leading off the seafront to connect with Northdown Road. In their heyday, all of them formed Cliftonville's busy hotel and guest house quarter during countless holiday seasons. In this 1920s view, a tram is trundling towards the town centre having turned off Cliff Terrace opposite the Clifton Baths. Athelstan Road gets its name from the Kentish hero who defeated the Danes in a naval battle in 851.

Frederick Lewis Pettman established his business in 1882, initially as a coal merchant, but soon branched into haulage and house removals. He had built the impressive depository in Athelstan Road by 1900. The Pettman name was already familiar in the town as his mother Charlotte ran the bathing station at Newgate Gap. His other business interests included Sunbeam Photography and the Kent Pure Ice Cream Company. Frederick Pettman became Mayor of Margate between 1932 and 1934, served as a magistrate and was a leading Freemason. Although he died on 16 December 1948, the company still exists operating to this day from the depository building.

Dalby Square was laid out in 1865 as a three sided square designed to minimise chilly winds coming off the North Sea on what had been a cornfield. It was named after Thomas Dalby Reeve, the local businessman who developed large parts of Cliftonville and later inspired 'Lord' George Sanger to set up his Hall By The Sea on Margate seafront. The view above dates from 1921.

Tennis courts and lawns were added to Dalby Square in 1885 and still looked pristine when this scene was recorded in the late 1920s as a publicity picture by operator Margate Estates, owner of Dreamland and the nearby Clifton Baths. The square offered sizeable homes and some became prep schools. The latter included Skelsmergh House School whose most famous pupil was author Dennis Wheatley who attended between 1905 and 1909. Note the boats which have been hand drawn into the background.

Cliftonville is unusual in having two impressive churches so close to each other. Both were built on the north side of what was then known as Alexandra Road in the latter years of the nineteenth century. The nearer, built in 1878, was originally a Wesleyan chapel and later became St Stephen's Methodist Church but today is St Michael & St Bishoy Coptic Orthodox Church. Beyond is St Paul's Church, which, with its vicarage, cost £8,500 to build in 1872. St Paul's became grade two listed in September 2010.

Pictured in 1913, Villette's tailor and hosiery shop at 49 Northdown Road would be a regular visit for shoppers for half a century. Countless youngsters were supplied with school uniforms as well as those for Scouts, Cubs, Guides and Brownies during that time. Straw boaters and panama hats feature prominently in the window so we can surmise this was taken during the summer.

Set on the corner with Harold Road at 199-203 Northdown Road, Reeve & Bayly's estate agency was one of several in the centre of Cliftonville and its premises are seen here during the mid 1930s. The firm also ran auctions, conducted valuations and collected rent for its clients. After the Second World War the business merged with another local agent to form Percy Gore, Reeve & Bayly and moved to offices further along Northdown Road, opposite the Methodist Church. The building became a café and health food store.

David Greig was a much-loved family owned chain of traditional upmarket grocery and delicatessen stores across south east England until taken over by Key Market in 1972. The branch at 141 Northdown Road was well staffed when this scene was recorded in the 1930s and freshly-starched aprons were the order of the day. Today, the premises are an independent butcher's shop.

Dreamland arranged for its sandwich men to be photographed by Edward Cox at his studio in Sweyn Road during 1930 before walking their beat to advertise Dare Devil Peggy, a one legged high diver who would plummet 60 feet, through flames, into a small tank of water. Cox was a prominent commercial photographer for decades and many early twentieth century images of the town were taken by him.

The 776 feet long German Graf Zeppelin LZ127 airship caused a sensation on 26 April 1930 when it flew over Wembley Stadium during the FA Cup final between Arsenal and Huddersfield. Its appearance over Cliftonville later the same day, while making its homeward journey, was greeted with similar incredulity by residents who gathered around RT Cullen's garage and petrol station in Sweyn Road.

Moylers is a name long associated with the shops of Cliftonville, the family having run a number of businesses here for nearly a century. Their first shop, a confectioner and tobacconist, was opened at 186 Northdown Road in 1928 and featured well-stocked display windows and external cabinets whose appearance helped cement the store's good reputation and attract affluent customers.

The outbreak of the Second World War would see several shops close for the duration along Northdown Road. Among them was housewares and chemist chain Timothy Whites whose premises at 190-192 were boarded up in 1940 as was neighbour Boots at 196-198. When Boots took over Timothy Whites in 1968, business here transferred to the latter's premises.

Cliftonville's answer to Harrod's was Bobby's department store at 220-228 Northdown Road. Arguably the centrepiece of the street, it was opened by Frederick Bobby c1888, one of nine branches he eventually owned around the country, including Margate, Tunbridge Wells and Torquay. He sold the company to the Draper's Trust in 1927, which later became the Debenham Group. The store was closed at the end of the January sales in 1973 and its loss has been lamented ever since. For many, this was the beginning of the end of civilised Cliftonville. Particularly well remembered are the Palm Court tearoom, with its own resident trio of musicians, and seasonal visits to see Father Christmas in the toy department.

This scene of a bustling Northdown Road in the 1920s looks towards Margate and gives us some idea of the length of the street. Dominating the skyline are the ornate pylons carrying the electrical wires of the Isle of Thanet Tramway. Although a double track here, the rails were too close to allow trams to pass one another, awkward if one met another coming the other way! Several delivery vans are parked either side of the road but one wagon, drawn by two horses, reminds us internal combustion hasn't taken over completely.

International Stores was a large grocery chain with the majority of its branches in southern England whose origins lay in tea importing. The staff of its shop at 239 Northdown Road, pictured in the 1920s, offered customers individual attention. Written orders could also be dropped off at the shop for later delivery by an errand boy on a bicycle. Although this branch had closed by the early 1970s, International survived until it was taken over by Gateway supermarkets in 1988.

Any signs of the trams have all but disappeared in this 1938 view of Northdown Road after the wires and rails were lifted the previous year to be replaced by East Kent buses. Floral Hall florist can be seen on the right hand side while further down is Munro Cobb, the four storey furniture shop from where flags are flying. The Kodak hoarding denotes Moyler's at the junction with Norfolk Road. Opposite, next door to Harrington's butcher, is Cuthbert's china shop while the family's hardware store is three doors further along.

Shell, National Benzole, Power and BP brands of petrol are on sale here. At the time, garages usually offered more than one brand to customers. Solus arrangements, where only one brand was sold, did not arrive until the 1950s. Naturally, a pump attendant served the petrol to customers.

These 1930s night time photos of Northdown Motor Company, set at the Northdown Road junction with Wyndham Avenue, show off the art deco styling of its forecourt extremely well.

New wire-wheeled Austins take pride of place in the showroom of the Northdown Motor Company c1928. Note the display of valve driven Pye radio sets, not for installing in the cars but for use in the home. It was common for garages, along with cycle shops and ironmongers, to sell domestic radios as they grew in popularity during the years before the Second World War.

The 1,305 seater Astoria Cinema, set on the western corner of Northdown Road with Wyndham Avenue, was officially opened on Saturday 4 August 1934 by screen stars of the day Jessie Matthews and Sonnie Hale who appeared in the film Evergreen, shown that evening. Designed in the art deco style of the period, the Astoria was built on the site of the former Palladium Garage in only 14 weeks by EA Stone. The cinema included an 18 feet deep stage, fronted by a three manual, five rank Compton organ, and a café. Thanks to a structural quirk, the projection box and screen were often shaken by the vibration of passing traffic. Sadly, the Astoria was badly damaged by a German bomb on 20 July 1940. It was further affected by three more raids later that year and what remained had to be demolished. A petrol station stands on the site today. The organ was transferred later by new owners ABC to its cinema in London's Stoke Newington where it was regularly played by Leslie Lawrence.

A long-time landmark of the Palm Bay end of Northdown Road was Ye Olde Charles Inn, built in 1926 by Russell's brewery of Gravesend and named after its architect, local man Charles Reeve. The pub catered for both local residents, who grew considerably in number after Palm Bay Estate was built opposite during the 1930s – when this image was captured – and holidaymakers staying nearby.

The Wheatsheaf, Nr Cliftonville.

The eastern area of Cliftonville was far leafier and almost traffic free when this rustic photo of the Wheatsheaf, looking along Northdown Park Road, was taken, possibly during the 1920s. Just beyond the cyclist, a car appears to be pulling out of Foreland Avenue. In the Victorian era, the Wheatsheaf proved popular as an excursion stop with horse brakes pulling up for afternoon teas.

The earliest mention of the Wheatsheaf, a classic flint-faced building, is recorded as 1733 and may well have been built by the local Cobb's Margate brewery whose lineage stretches back even further. Whitbread Fremlins would have taken on the place as part of its acquisition of Cobb's in January 1968. The building was extended in 1975 to become a Beefeater restaurant before being sold during the 1980s to Suffolk based Greene King who absorbed the place into its Hungry Horse restaurant chain.

From chemist's apprentice to gangbuster

One day in October 1929, under the watchful eye of the senior pharmacist, an 18 year old apprentice dispenser carefully made up a prescription of arsenic for the mother of the smartly dressed man facing them across the counter in the Cliftonville branch of Boots the Chemist.

The 196-198 Northdown Road branch of Boots the Chemist, seen here c1930, was where an apprentice dispenser made up a bottle of arsenic for murderer Sidney Fox.

There was nothing particularly unusual in prescribing arsenic in those days for, in well-diluted quantities, the strong poison was held to have properties which would ease digestion, allergies and sleep disorders. It had proved a particularly popular tonic in Victorian times.

A few days later, the man's mother, Mrs Rosaline Fox, was found dead in room 66 of the Metropole Hotel, Margate (Turner Contemporary stands on the site today) and was at first thought to have suffocated following a fire in the room. Suspicions grew though when her son Sidney tried to claim against two life insurance policies he had taken out on Rosaline just a few days earlier. He was soon charged with her murder – it was a case that shocked the nation.

The cause of Rosaline's death turned out to be strangulation (her body was exhumed a week after burial) but it was while preparing his desperate defence, that Fox claimed she was poisoned by a wrongly dispensed dose of arsenic.

The police visited Boots in Northdown Road to check the prescription log and it was famous pathologist Sir Bernard Spilsbury who disproved Fox's allegation. Fox was found guilty and hanged at Maidstone prison in January 1930.

But what happened to the teenage dispenser though? The events left their mark on him in a remarkable way and it would not be the last time the young man came face to face with a murderer.

Far from it, for four years later Ernest Millen, who had grown up in Westgate, replied to an advert

In retirement in Birchington, Ernest Millen shows off an original cartoon by Carl Giles of the Daily Express which used to hang in his Scotland Yard office.

to join the Metropolitan Police. He was one of only 20 to be taken on from a batch of 180 applicants and, having signed up for a 30 year tenure, he became police officer number 123557 just a month after his 23rd birthday.

Millen quickly proved himself a capable officer and by 1938, at the age of 26, was a full detective in London's East End.

During what can be rightly described as a highly successful career, Millen rose through the ranks to become a Deputy Assistant Commissioner of the Metropolitan Police. Ultimately holding the rank of Commander, he was in charge of, at different times, the Fraud Squad and the more famous Flying Squad, based at Scotland Yard.

Records show that at a time in the early and mid 1960s when Scotland Yard was scandalised by corrupt officers taking bribes from criminals, Millen was one of the honest men who helped to flush out the bent coppers and restore the force's good name.

Millen earned himself a reputation as a gangbuster, ultimately responsible for the successful operations that brought down the Kray twins, the Richardson gang and, in 1963, which rounded up several of the Great Train Robbers.

When he retired in 1968, plaudits and thanks came from afar. J Edgar Hoover, the head of the FBI, was among many well-wishers. Hoover told him: "I have learned of your forthcoming retirement and want to express my appreciation for the cooperation and assistance you have furnished to my associates over the years.

"Organisations having your caliber of men are richly endowed and I am certain you will be able to look back with great pride on your accomplishments."

It is unlikely the criminals which 'Millen of the Yard' brought to justice would have shared those sentiments!

In the early 1970s Millen wrote of his exploits in a book entitled Specialist In Crime. Unsurprisingly, Millen was contemptuous of the criminals he encountered. He described East End based Ronnie and Reggie Kray as "a couple of thugs without even the wit to cover up their tracks."

The Krays, brother Charles, centre, is flanked by twins Reginald, left, and Ronald in the mid 1960s. The twins would later spend the rest of their lives in jail.

He said: "When it came to the crunch they were hopelessly incompetent, even as murderers. Reginald Kray, when he tried to shoot Jack 'the hat' McVitie in 1967, found the gun he proudly toted around wouldn't even work. It took both brothers and another man to shove a carving knife into their victim. It would be comical, if it were not so messy and bloody."

South of the Thames, the Richardson brothers, Charles

and Edward, with their gang of hoodlums had taken over a night club in Catford from where they ran drugs and protection rackets. A gun battle with the Krays at Mr Smith's club in March 1966 marked the beginning of the end for the gang, said Millen. At last there was enough evidence to arrest and charge them with a range of offences by July that year.

Transgressors of the brothers had been sadistically tortured – often by pulling out victims' teeth with pliars, being nailed to the floor or cutting off their toes. Eventually, after a 46 day trial in spring 1967, in which many victims finally found the courage to speak, the gangsters were jailed, Charles for 25 years and Edward for 10.

Millen was awarded the CBE in 1968 for his loyal service and moved, with his wife Ena, to Birchington the following year.

Taking on the Mafia doesn't feature in many people's retirement plans but that is what happened when he became a security consultant to the Grand Met Hotel group for a time, advising the company about how to prevent the organised crime syndicate from infiltrating its gaming operations.

In Birchington, the one time apprentice chemist is perhaps best remembered as a leading light of the horticultural society – Millen particularly enjoyed growing roses in his front garden – and the local Rotary Club. He died in July 1988, aged 77.

In May 1965, Ernest Millen made a plea for information about three of the Great Train Robbers, Bruce Reynolds, Charlie Wilson and James White, on international TV via the Early Bird satellite.

Sunbeam summer times made us smile

In the days when nobody had a camera of their own, being able to take home a photo of you and your family or friends enjoying a day at the seaside was a souvenir worth having.

During the summer holiday season, queues of people would form outside wooden huts at all of Thanet's main beaches to see photos taken the day before by strolling beach photographers. If people liked them, they invariably bought them and perhaps ordered extras to send to friends.

The company behind this major operation of logistics,

Sunbeam's Sweyn Road premises were behind the Cameo Cinema. Right: Photographer with hefty reflex camera.

rapid mechanized processing and photographic skill was Sunbeam Photography, whose head office and laboratories were to be found at 82 Sweyn Road, Cliftonville.

Sunbeam was established shortly after the First World War – although its founder John Milton Worssell had been taking photos in the area since 1912. In 1919, Worssell took on a photographer's concession along part of Margate's foreshore during the summer season. It would prove to be the start of something big.

By this time, a war weary population was eager to enjoy itself after four years of hardship and sorrow. Combine this with less formality around bathing in the sea and a greater willingness to have a photo taken and you have a recipe for success.

Business grew rapidly between 1919 and 1939, while for those taking the pictures, the equipment became lighter too. Heavy field cameras, mounted on tripods, using delicate glass plate negatives gave way to hand-held bespoke designed cameras which took enough roll film for 100 postcard sized pictures at a time before reloading.

There was already a portrait studio at 156 Northdown Road but by 1925, the volume of work had grown sufficiently for Worssell to build and equip his new head office and labs at Sweyn Road

Above and left: Holidaymakers enjoying differing styles of fun along the foreshore were the hallmark of pre-war pictures.

costing £5,000. The building provided developing and printing facilities, retouching, picture framing and camera building and maintenance for the next half century.

Beach photography would continue to play an important part in the Sunbeam business for decades, the simple belief being that the more pictures were taken, the more likely a sale would be made. By the end of the summer season in 1939, some 47 photographers were working patches along promenades, piers and beaches – a few braving it into the sea to get their shots – along the Thanet coastline, which naturally included Cliftonville. Between them all they could take up to 35,000 photos in a day. One photographer, working the sands of Ramsgate, actually managed 3,000 shots by himself one August Bank Holiday in the late 1930s.

Worssell's two sons, Richard and Jack, joined him in the business during the years before the Second World War and would take a greater hand in operations as the years progressed.

Sunbeam was branching out in other directions as well. It had already established a successful wedding and portrait business through its studio. The latter catered for animals as well as human subjects. Skilled retouchers could, at a customer's request, enhance pet portraits by painting in glasses, a hat or a scarf around the animal's neck.

Margate and Cliftonville, with so many larger hotels to offer, was a popular choice for national conferences of political parties, trades unions and voluntary organisations. It was this circuit that Sunbeam targeted next. Hundreds, if not thousands, of photos were taken at these events and willingly snapped up by delegates. In years to follow, Sunbeam photographers found themselves regularly travelling to Brighton, Folkestone or Eastbourne to cover conferences, such was the company's reputation.

Sunbeam photographers had a wide range of props to use at its beach stations including, by the early 1960s, a rather tired, but still popular, cow at Margate's Sun Deck.

With hostilities over in 1945, Sunbeam resumed its operations along the coast as visitors flocked to the area to enjoy themselves. Schools work became an added area of expertise for the photographers, using panoramic cameras to record large groups of several hundred children. A camera would rotate on a tripod taking in a semi-circular group – some mischievous youngsters at one end of the shot would run around the back of the group to appear a second time as the camera caught up with them!

By the early 1950s, Leica half frame 35mm cameras were becoming available and quickly caught on with Sunbeam. These cameras were able to take 72 photos on a roll of standard 36 exposure film – offering a great cost saving in materials without loss of picture quality. Initially, Sunbeam used Leicas for conference work but such was their success that other half frame cameras, mainly the Olympus Pen, were bought for those working the foreshore areas and, just as often, the pleasure steamers plying off Margate and Ramsgate. A day trip on board

The Royal Daffodil was a regular visitor to Margate, taking passengers for no-passport trips to France – and Sunbeam would be on board to record the day. Naturally, this image of Royal Daffodil at sea was taken by one of its photographers. The ship had a distinguished war record, rescuing 9,500 men from the beaches of Dunkirk in May 1940.

either the Royal Sovereign, Royal Daffodil or Crested Eagle was not complete without having your picture taken by one of the Sunbeam team.

That team, at the height of the booming 1950s summers, could swell to 300 strong. Many of these summer casual employees were students who were all given basic training in how to use the cameras and handle people effectively. Subjects needed to almost fill

Between the late 1950s and mid 1970s Volkswagen had its UK base at Ramsgate importing complete cars and spare parts. Left: Sunbeam set up this photo to show what went into a Beetle and right: Marking the 100,000th car imported via Ramsgate.

the frame and once the focus had been manually adjusted to appear sharp in the viewfinder, that was the moment to press the shutter button.

Worssell and his sons continued to run the business, father still being involved when he was in his eighties and only giving up after his wife's death. Worssell himself died in May 1973.

By the early 1970s technical advances in chemistry and machinery had enabled colour processing to become cost-effective for a mass audience and Sunbeam responded accordingly, upgrading the equipment at Sweyn Road.

The same technical advances though now brought colour photography into the hands of the individual with the arrival of easy to use Kodak Instamatic cameras, cartridge film and fast mail order processing. All of this took away a slice of Sunbeam's market – why pay someone else to take your photo when you can take it so easily yourself? Another key factor was the growing number of holidaymakers travelling abroad for guaranteed summer sunshine. Far fewer people were buying Sunbeam photos from the beachside huts.

Richard and Jack Worssell were now both in their 60s

and looking to retire. Without anybody in the family wanting to take on the operation, they decided to sell up to United Photographic Laboratories in 1976.

The new owner saw no future in beach photos and concerned itself only with the schools work. Equipment at Sweyn Road was transferred elsewhere and the premises were sold.

Perhaps most enduring of Sunbeam's work has proved to be its commercial photography. The local councils of Thanet, along with Dreamland, the Lido and many other businesses as well as the local papers in the area, regularly commissioned Sunbeam to take pictures for holiday guides, promotional brochures,

Until closure in the 1970s Sunbeam had purpose built huts on Thanet's beaches to enable people to view and buy photos. This one was located on the prom at Westbrook.

Chief photographer at Sunbeam's closure was stalwart Chris Fright, seen here in 1986, who enjoyed a freelance career which included filming local news for BBC and ITV with his Swiss-made Paillard Bolex 16mm ciné camera.

reports, special events and visits by a variety of the great and good.

All of that work has helped build a unique record of the history of Thanet. Happily, a good proportion of it has survived and in more recent times has been carefully archived with the help of Canterbury Christ Church University, supported by Heritage Lottery funding.

Only the best places for happy holidays

Boasting no fewer than 200 bedrooms, the Cliftonville Hotel was the first to be built in the town and dates from 1868, the heyday of the area's development. Sited in a prime spot on Ethelbert Crescent overlooking the sea, it catered very much for the Victorian wealthy middle and upper classes who didn't want to holiday in lower class Margate. Maintaining a reputation for top quality, the hotel had no real competition until the Queen's was built some 20 years later. Despite great changes after the First World War, the Cliftonville still merited five stars in the Automobile Association's members' guide of 1938 when a double room cost between 21 and 25 shillings (£1.05 to £1.25) per night. In the 1960s, the site was redeveloped as a ten pin bowling alley, flats and latterly a night club.

The Cliftonville Hydro Hotel, in Cliftonville Avenue, is believed to have been built in 1920. Offering 80 rooms and parking nearby for 30 cars, it specialised in what was then considered to be a full range of health improving treatments for adults and children. The building included an extension with a yellow tile hung frontage, partially obscured by trees in this late 1930s photograph.

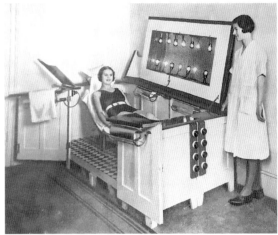

Above: Turkish baths, top right: An electric bath – forerunner of the sunbed, perhaps – and, right: What appears to be a roomful of instruments for torturing small children, more likely bright sun lamps, were among the facilities on offer at the Hydro during the inter-wars era. Other treatments included the use of steam, seaweed, Vichy, Russian, medicated pine and foam baths.

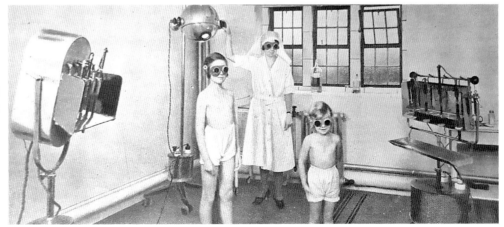

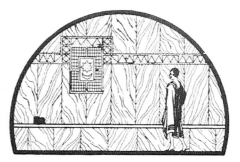

FOR comfort, pleasure and restfulness in Margate's wonderful air, the Hydro is unsurpassed. It is a model of unostentatious efficiency. Central heating. H. & C. Water in all bedrooms. Lift, etc.

Situated on high ground in the residential part of Cliftonville, yet is close to sea and amusements.

THE HYDRO BATHS

which include Turkish, Russian, Electric and Medical, are judged to be the finest in the country.

A fully Illustrated Booklet of the Hydro, the Hydro Baths, or both, post free

THE HYDRO

Cliftonville Avenue, Cliftonville

Telephone:	*Telegrams:*
MARGATE 584	" HYDRO, MARGATE."

New signage was installed over the Hydro's front entrance during the 1930s, perhaps suggesting a change of ownership. In keeping with its emphasis on good health, the premises were alcohol free while, in 1938, a double room for the night would set back guests between 12 and 16 shillings (60p to 80p). The building still stands but has become apartments in more recent times. The adjoining tile hung building is now home to an art gallery, having been offices in the 1980s and 1990s.

CLIFTONVILLE COURT HOTEL, CLIFTONVILLE
TELEPHONE 509 MARGATE

Fronting Lewis Crescent and overlooking Walpole Bay was Cliftonville Court Hotel. This promotional postcard was used in September 1923 and an arrow has been helpfully added to point out the place. A stroll along what was renamed Prince's Walk later in the decade would have appealed to many of Cliftonville Court's guests. During the mid 1950s, the hotel was one of a cluster in the vicinity to be purchased by holiday camp king Billy Butlin.

At the opposite end of the block to Cliftonville Court Hotel was the Endcliffe Hall Hotel which opened for business in 1899. Its 80 bedrooms offered comfortable, modestly priced three star accommodation, a week's stay costing six guineas (£6.30) in the high season of 1938. After laying empty for some time in the early 21st century, the Endcliffe was badly damaged by a spectacular fire in May 2005. Nearly 100 firefighters came from across east Kent to put out the flames. The building has been replaced by apartments.

HOTEL FLORENCE.

Lewis Avenue and Cornwall Gardens, CLIFTONVILLE.

This Hotel is situated right on the sea front, facing the Queen's Promenade, commanding one of the finest positions in Cliftonville. Magnificently Furnished throughout with every convenience.

Grand Lounge
Drawing Room
Reading and Writing Room
  BEST ENGLISH MEAT.

Dining Room to seat 100
Billiard Room (full-sized table)
Electric Light
  EXCELLENT CUISINE.

TERMS EN PENSION FROM 2 GUINEAS PER WEEK

Tariff on application from

Telephone 118.
Telegrams: "Hotel Florence, Margate."

Mrs. Jamieson (née BOWMAN)
Late of Dalby Square.   Proprietress.

Standing on the corner of Cornwall Gardens and what was then known as Lewis Avenue (later Eastern Esplanade) was the Hotel Florence, built in 1913 by Florence Bowman, who was already a successful landlady based in Dalby Square. The hotel had 120 bedrooms and was designed by Thomas Wallis, a partner of the architectural practice which later designed the impressive Hoover building in west London. The hotel continued to be independently run for many years and by the late 1930s had three star accreditation from the AA when prices for a double room varied between 12 and 21 shillings per night (60p and £1.05).

St Georges Hotel Cliftonville, N° 12733.

Long before it became a bastion of Butlin's offerings in Cliftonville, the St George's Hotel offered quality accommodation for its guests in all 130 of its rooms and by 1938 had four stars from the AA to show for that. Its wide frontage overlooking the bowling greens on the esplanade made it a tricky subject to picture head on. The side angle chosen by this postcard photographer offers the chance to marvel at an old car in the left hand corner, probably the only one parked for some distance.

The four storey Norfolk Hotel, fronting Norfolk Road and Eastern Esplanade, on the block next to the St George's Hotel would also form part of Butlin's presence in Cliftonville from the mid 1950s. Until then it was operated by the Nicholson Group as a four star hotel with 120 bedrooms. Typically, in the late 1930s, a week's stay at the Norfolk would range between five and seven guineas (£5.25 and £7.35) according to season and demand while evening dinner was six shillings and sixpence (33p).

GRAND HOTEL, CLIFTONVILLE, MARGATE.

Edward Cox (Photo) Margate.

Built in 1899 and originally named the Cliftonville Hydro Hotel, its name was changed in 1920 to the Grand Hotel – the original name then being taken by another establishment across town. The building now has four storeys of additional rooms above the café and ballroom. This Edward Cox image may well have been taken to mark the new name and revised look.

Dalmeny Hotel, Cliftonville, Margate.

At first glance, it's hard to understand whereabouts the Dalmeny Hotel was in Cliftonville. However, sight of the Newgate Gap Bridge to the left of the building in this 1907 postcard – it's the original bridge and would be replaced by a new one that same year – tells us it was on Ethelbert Crescent. The Dalmeny would later be absorbed into the Queen's Highcliffe Hotel. The Dalmeny building dated from 1885 and had previously been a girls' school.

The Queen's Hotel was one of three establishments forming a large block, the others being Kimber's Hotel, in the centre, and the Highcliffe Hotel on the seaward end (left portion). Seen from Ethelbert Crescent in this early Edwardian view, a domed section was added later to the Queen's Hotel end to link it to the former Dalmeny Hotel. Mrs Campion, owner of the Highcliffe, took over Kimber's and merged with both Queen's and Dalmeny to form the Queen's Highcliffe Hotel. It soon became one of the most prestigious hotels on the south coast.

Formally dressed Edwardian ladies and gentlemen fill the large Tudor dining room of the Queen's Highcliffe Hotel in this contemporary artistic postcard. The hotel offered 200 bedrooms, all with hot and cold water, and competed directly with the Cliftonville Hotel, a short distance along the esplanade. By 1938, both establishments had been awarded five stars by the AA.

QUEEN'S HOTEL AND OVAL BANDSTAND, CLIFTONVILLE.

The Queen's Highcliffe provides a splendid backdrop to the Oval bandstand and its lawns in this 1924 view. We can clearly see the domed section added just 13 years before which would remain a feature of the building until its eventual demise in 1978, 10 years after being sold off by Butlin's to Louis Holloway who opened a dolphinarium here. Hotels of this size would characterise seaside resorts around Britain as they saw a gradual decline in fortunes with the arrival of foreign package holidays in the decades to follow.

"BEULAH"
ATHELSTAN R.d CLIFTONVILLE. MARGATE.

Staying in a five star hotel was simply beyond the reach of many people who opted for more modest lodgings in one of dozens of guest or boarding houses spread out across Cliftonville. As photography became popular so began a tradition for local snappers to visit each week to gather the guests for a group picture, copies of which were swiftly provided as souvenirs to take home.

No 27 **Stanmore   Athelston Rd. Cliftonville, Margate**

Have these people just arrived for a Cliftonville holiday in the charabancs or are they about to go on a day excursion around the local countryside? We shall never know but the Stanmore Boarding House in Athelstan Road (note spelling in the picture!) clearly did good business by putting them up for their stay at the seaside in the early years of the twentieth century.

GLENWOOD BOARDING ESTABLISHMENT
EDGAR ROAD. CLIFTONVILLE.

Set in Edgar Road was, and still is, the Glenwood, seen in this 1915 view as a boarding house. Aimed squarely at the bucket and spade trade in the summer season, it catered for a clientele of modest means. It wouldn't be until after the Second World War that it moved upmarket to provide the full facilities of a hotel and became a popular venue for weddings and dinner dances.

GLENWOOD, EDGAR RD. CLIFTONVILLE. MARGATE.

Smartly attired for their group photo taken at the beginning of what would hopefully be a memorable holiday in Cliftonville are these guests staying at the Glenwood, sometime in the late 1920s or early 1930s. Virtually everyone is looking to the camera and seemingly ready to enjoy themselves.

A favourite caption for photographers to add to hotel group pictures like this was 'Just a line from....' with the relevant hotel or town name added before printing postcard copies. The idea was, of course, that guests would send home these images to family and friends during their stay. In this case it's 1920s holidaymakers staying at The Gables Hotel in Norfolk Road forming a line.

NORTHDOWN HALL, NORFOLK ROAD, CLIFTONVILLE.

"South Block"   "The Lodge" in the background   "North Block."

Northdown Hall Hotel in Norfolk Road was a sizeable establishment set over two blocks on either side of the junction with Cumberland Road. When the advert, top, appeared and photos for a brochure were taken c1930, it offered no fewer than 100 bedrooms. The advert highlights a new lounge and verandah as well as a free billiards room. All meat served in its impressive dining room was best English. By 1938 a week's stay at the hotel would have cost between three and six guineas (£3.15 and £6.30) according to the time of year.

Warwick Road, Cliftonville.

Most of the roads leading off the Northdown Road shopping area to the seafront would have looked similar to this inter-wars era scene of Warwick Road. The majority of the properties were guest houses or private hotels, often family run, with a landlady at the helm in day to day charge. It was an unwise person who upset a seaside landlady – the managements of the Lido and Winter Gardens summer shows understood this golden rule, ensuring these redoubtable folk were first to see their performers and went away with a good impression!

Surrey Road, Cliftonville.

As you walk down Warwick Road towards the sea, the street turns into Surrey Road and again this serene, uncluttered view dates from between the two world wars. The properties were first built at the turn of the nineteenth and twentieth centuries as spacious villas, yet lent themselves to easily becoming guest houses once holidays with pay became more widespread.

Thought to be one of the first steel girder construction buildings in Kent when erected during the mid 1930s, the art deco style Northumberland Hotel, facing the sea at Palm Bay, represented a modern take on a luxurious place in which to stay.

Catering mainly for a Jewish clientele, the Northumberland proved popular in the years leading up to the Second World War until requisitioned by the military as a convalescent home.

After the war ended, the hotel continued to specialise in Kosher cuisine until the mid 1950s when the owners decided to turn the place into apartments, renaming it Northumberland Court. The ground floor bar remained open to the public as a separate entity for many years after.

Today, apartments are keenly sought after and the freeholding company works hard to maintain high standards of care and maintenance around the building.

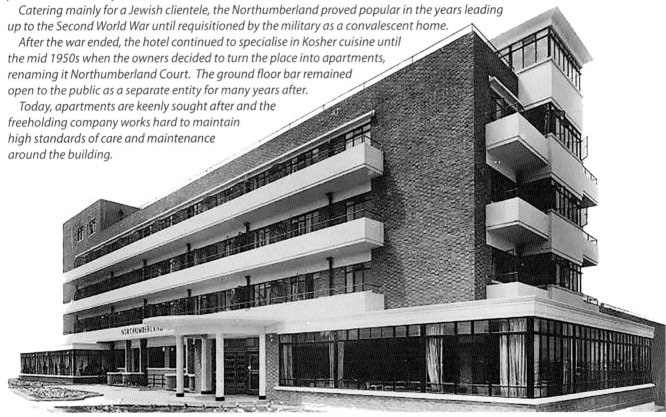

The art deco influence of the Northumberland Hotel is evident in all three of these illustrations.
Top: One of the upper floor landings.
Top right: The lounge bar which featured wood panelling repurposed from the liner RMS Mauritania, scrapped in 1935. Right: The hotel's writing room was, no doubt, a quiet place in which to write correspondence and read books or newspapers.

Cliftonville – a cradle of beauty contests

The story of Cliftonville is closely linked with that of the purpose-built seaside resort as smart hotels and shops sprang up on virgin land from around 1860 onwards.

Some 70 years later Cliftonville found itself at the forefront of the new concept of the beauty contest. It was one of the first places in Britain to see these events bursting onto an unsuspecting public as weekly competitions were held beside the town's Clifton Baths open air swimming pool.

The summer of 1930 was a long and hot one, bringing ideal weather for the events to be watched with enthusiasm by an audience becoming captivated by Hollywood style glamour. Beauty contests were regarded as something modern and exciting. The earliest competitors lining up in these parades were mainly female holidaymakers entering for a lark and were delighted if they came away with a box of chocolates.

From 1949 comes this long line up of bathing beauties ready to parade around the open air swimming pool at the Lido in a weekly contest. Most appear to be entering for fun.

A compere of those early parades was Eric Iles, who would eventually become Chairman and managing director of Margate Estates, the holding company which owned the Lido and Dreamland.

Years later, he recalled that in the 1930s many of the contestants hired swimsuits for use at the pool, either from the baths or the nearby Pettman's bathing station at Newgate Gap.

Made from a standard blue serge with the pool's name emblazoned across the front, these costumes did little to flatter a young woman's figure! The only thing different about the outfits was the sizes – large, medium or small. On the other hand the top prizes were more fashionable bathing costumes presented by a well known manufacturer.

It should be said that women were, by and large, no longer afraid of showing more than an ankle at the seaside and the contests were considered trendy. In those early years, said Iles, having more than 50 girls step up for a parade was quite common.

After the Second World War, young women became more competition conscious, more concerned about general standards of beauty, with some feeling they could not stand out against prettier faces, or those with striking figures.

Judges changed over time too. Originally, they were nearly always women – three would be invited from the audience, but it was found women were too analytical.

In the post war era, including a theme to a Lido contest brought variety. Here, majorette style hats and and a baton for the leader added some colour and encouraged poise.

Lido contestants were given grass skirts for Miss South Seas Siren events held during the 1950s.

Winners of a weekly Lido line up would often kneel on a rostrum rather than stand on it for a more flattering pose.

After 1945 judges were almost always men and there would often be a showbiz personality on hand as well to help decide who was going to get the sash and prizes.

The Lido's beauty contests developed and, week by week, they featured different aspects of female charm. Typical titles were Miss Physical Excellence, Miss Calf & Ankle, Miss Lovely Legs, Miss Sports Girl, Miss Mermaid and Miss Grace & Bearing. During the 1950s Miss South Seas Siren was another title which saw contestants sashaying around the pool wearing grass skirts over their costumes.

The organisers found if young women wore ballet type skirts over costumes they could be unbuttoned to enable judges to concentrate on looking at legs without being influenced by pretty faces. In some contests, girls actually wore hoods over their heads, giving them a Ku Klux Klan appearance!

Poise and colour could be achieved by handing out majorette style hats to be worn with a baton for the leader. Adding spectacle and balance, girls in the Grace & Bearing contest were given Grecian urns with which to parade around the pool. Vital statistics

Hoods were sometimes worn by Miss Lovely Legs contestants so that judges would not be distracted by a pretty face.

The title of Miss Margate 1960 was won by Joyce Cooke from Kilburn.

were the vogue of the beauty parade too but there is no record of the measurements of the first girl to win at the Lido. In those far off days no one dared to ask!

With television catching on during the 1950s, beauty contests gained in international popularity – the Miss

World competition proving the pinnacle of pageants for the next three decades at least. Closer to home, Margate Corporation decided that hosting regional heats – and ultimately the grand finals – of the National Bathing Beauty contest would bring valuable publicity to the town.

Above: Hughie Greene of Opportunity Knocks fame congratulates the winners of a Miss Margate heat held at Cliftonville's Oval in 1963.

Left: TV musician and comedian Roy Castle no doubt enjoyed his celebrity status when asked to judge contests in the 1960s.

After all, Fleet Street papers and TV were falling over each other to get photos of the young women taking part.

Cliftonville's Oval began hosting heats for the first time in 1960 and it was Joyce Cooke, a blue-eyed blonde, from Kilburn in north London, who won her way to become Miss Margate and represent the town in the national finals. Not to be confused with the Miss Margate carnival queen – although plenty were – contestants were attracted from far and near for the town's competitions over the following eight years. Sadly no local girl won the council-backed title which offered £200 first and £100 second prizes.

Cliftonville, not to be outshone by Margate, had its own annual beauty contest for several years. Anne Godfrey was Miss Cliftonville in 1968.

Margate girl Jill Kemp was winner of the Rothmans Miss Lido title in 1974.

In 1965 Southern Television, the ITV franchise holder of the day, decided to move its own contest from Bognor Regis to Margate where it stayed for four more seasons before shifting to Southend.

These contests not only brought competitors from afar but celebrity judges including, at different times, Hughie Green of TV's Opportunity Knocks fame, singer Adam Faith in summer season at Margate Winter Gardens in 1964, bus driver turned crooner Matt Monro, musician Roy Castle, newspaper

A long line of beauties takes to the catwalk of Cliftonville's Oval for the Margate Corporation sponsored Miss Margate title in 1968. Owing to cost cutting measures this event turned out to be the last one run by the council.

columnist Marjorie Proops and stage artiste Danny La Rue, Margate's summer show star of 1968.

That 1968 event would prove to be the final of finals with the realisation that fashions were changing while cuts to public spending meant that costs and prize money were harder to justify.

A story in the Isle of Thanet Gazette from September 1968 headlined the announcement of the contest's end with the headline 'Margate takes the cheesecake off menu' saying it was farewell to the cry of 36-23-36 along with oft-repeated ambitions to travel the world and meet people.

A platform and catwalk has been built out into the Lido pool for the 1973 Miss Rothmans contest. The compere here is Tony Savage, familiar to many as the Lido pleasure centre's organist.

Back at the Lido, weekly contests continued throughout the 1970s and were now being supported by sponsors. Among them was tobacco manufacturer Rothman's who, in the early part of the decade, held a gala day there with its own flying aerobatic team passing overhead for a half hour long display. The last time costume-clad young women paraded around the pool was in 1981, fitting in a final season before the Lido site was sold by owners Associated Leisure. How tastes have changed – smoking sponsorship has been outlawed and beauty parades have long been considered demeaning and politically incorrect.

Acknowledgements

The author would like to thank the following for their invaluable help:

Ms Susannah Foad and Mr Jerry Pitcher for allowing the use of the majority of the photographs included in this book, taken from their respective photograph and postcard collections.

With thanks also to the following for the use of their photographs on these pages:
Thanet Hidden History Facebook page 35, 70, 90 top, 97, 98 & 99 left;
Margate Museum 41, 42, 48 left and 50; The John T Williams Collection 67, 123 left and 127;
The Mick Twyman Collection, via Susannah Foad 79; Mr Matt Morris 80 & 81;
SEAS Heritage Collection © Thanet District Council 91, 93, 94, 95 left, 121, 122 and 124 left.

All other photographs © Bill Evans Collection.

Further reading about the history of Cliftonville is readily available from the Margate Civic Society website, www.margatecivicsociety.org.uk. The society holds regular meetings and welcomes new members. The Facebook pages Margate & Local Family History, Thanet Hidden History and Cliftonville Nostalgia all share many photographs. Visit www.grasscliftonville.org for updates on its community projects.

Bibliography

Numerous cuttings and other items held by the Bill Evans Collection from publications including:
Isle of Thanet Gazette, Thanet Times, East Kent Times, Kent Life, Bygone Kent and Margate Civic Society's newsletters.

We have taken all reasonable steps to ensure the correct people are credited for their photographs but any issues can be addressed to bygonepublishing@gmail.com and amendments will be considered for any future editions.